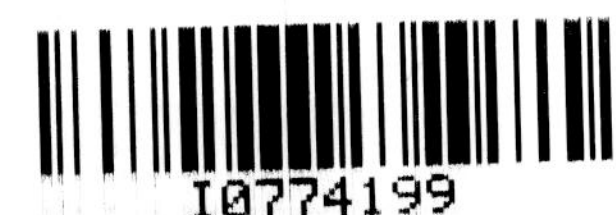

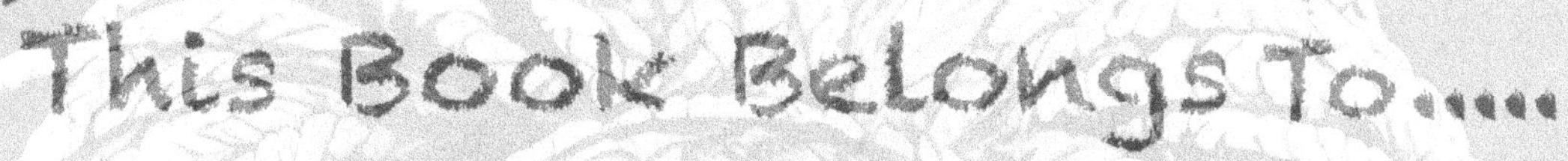

This Book Belongs To.....

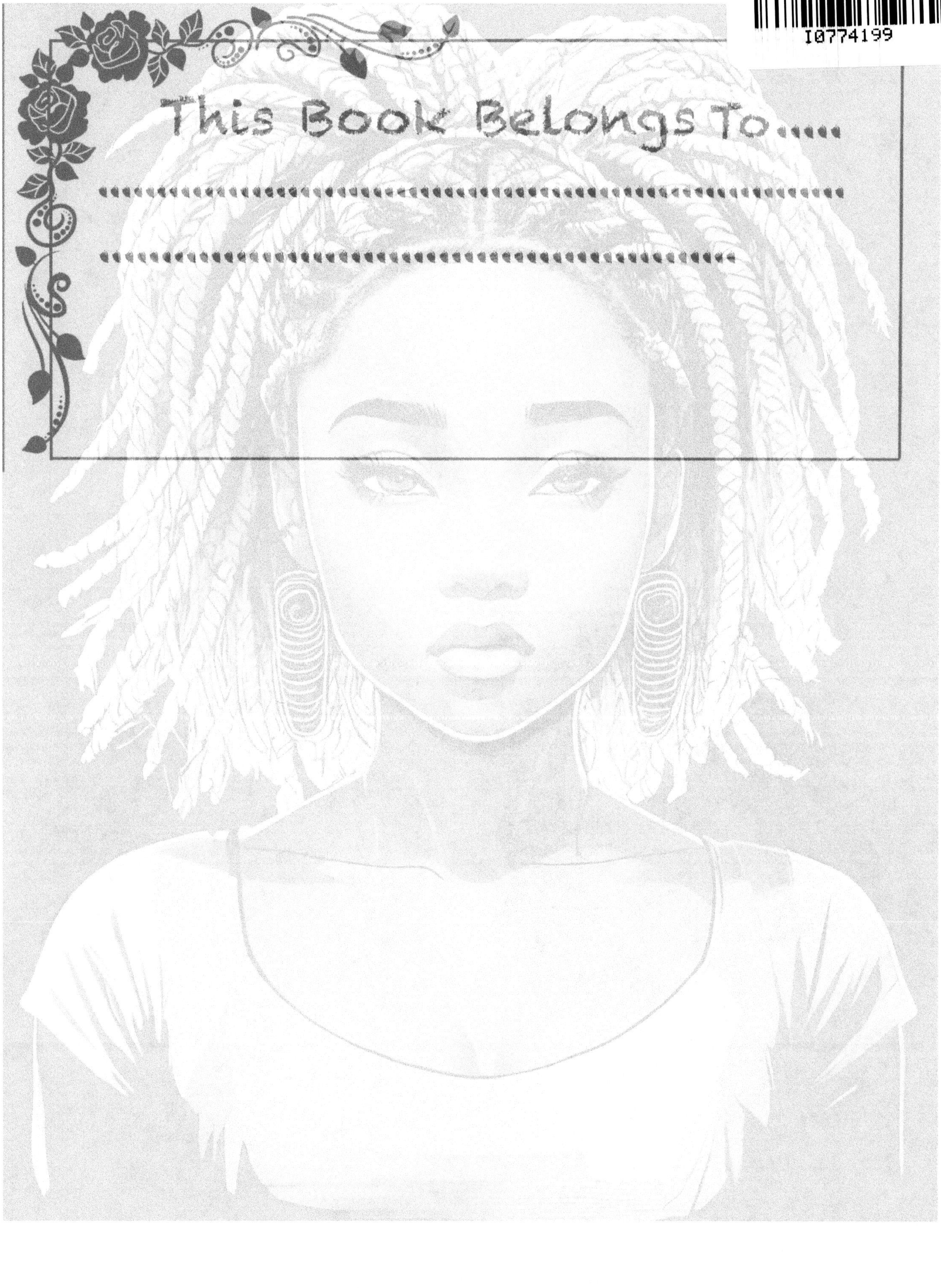

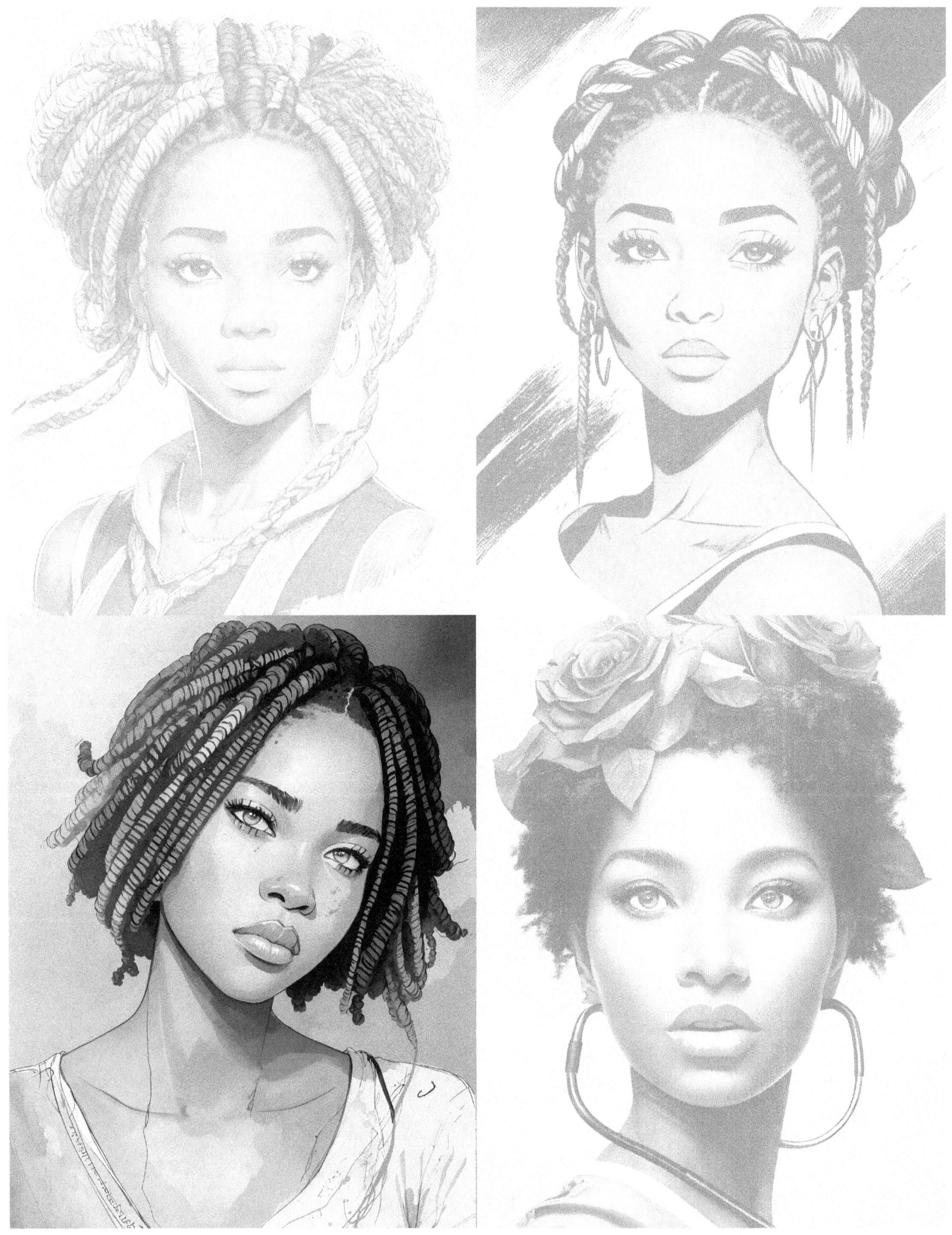

BLACK WOMEN GRAYSCALE

Copyright: Published in the United States
Published 2024
MOO MOO PINK

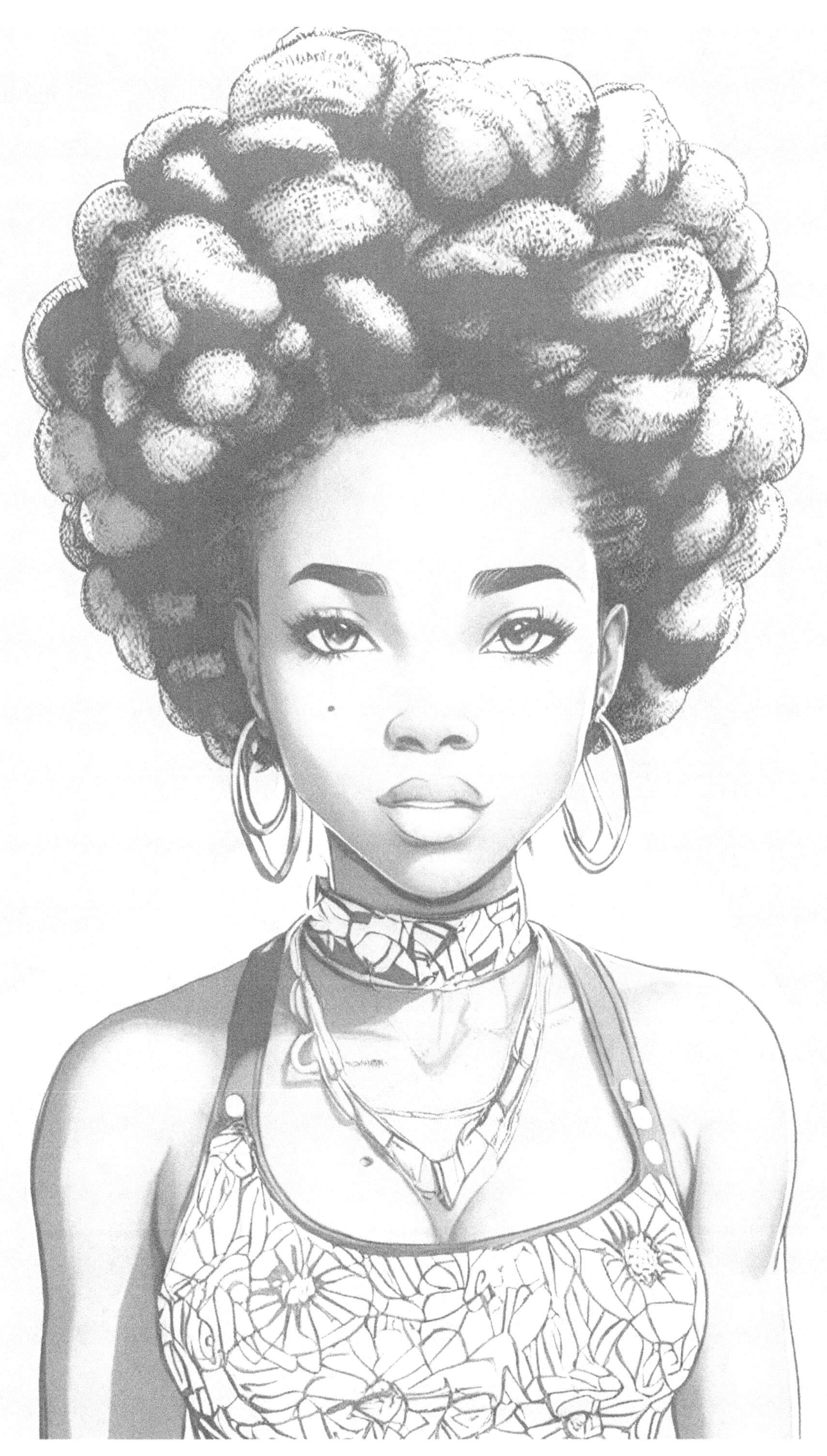

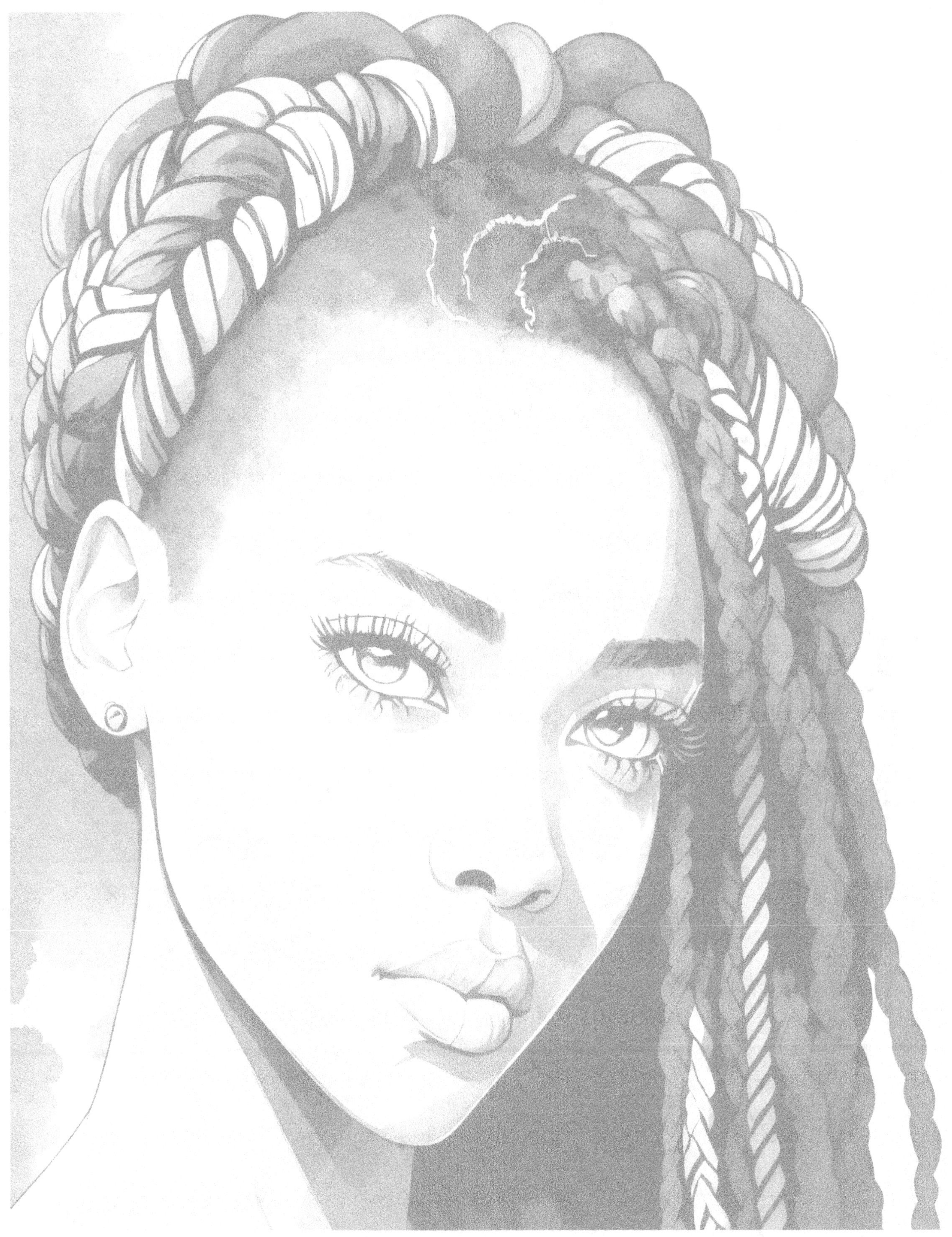

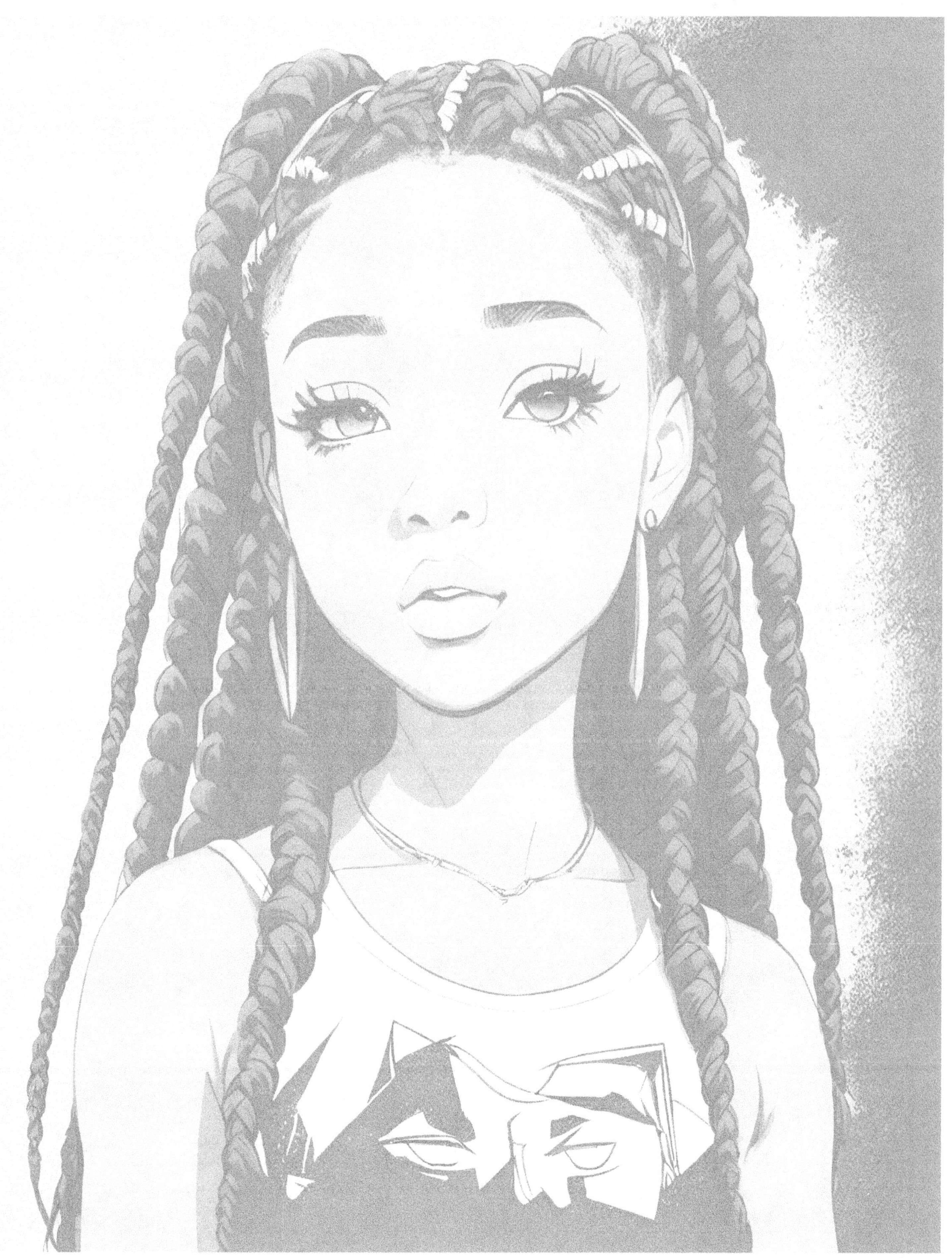

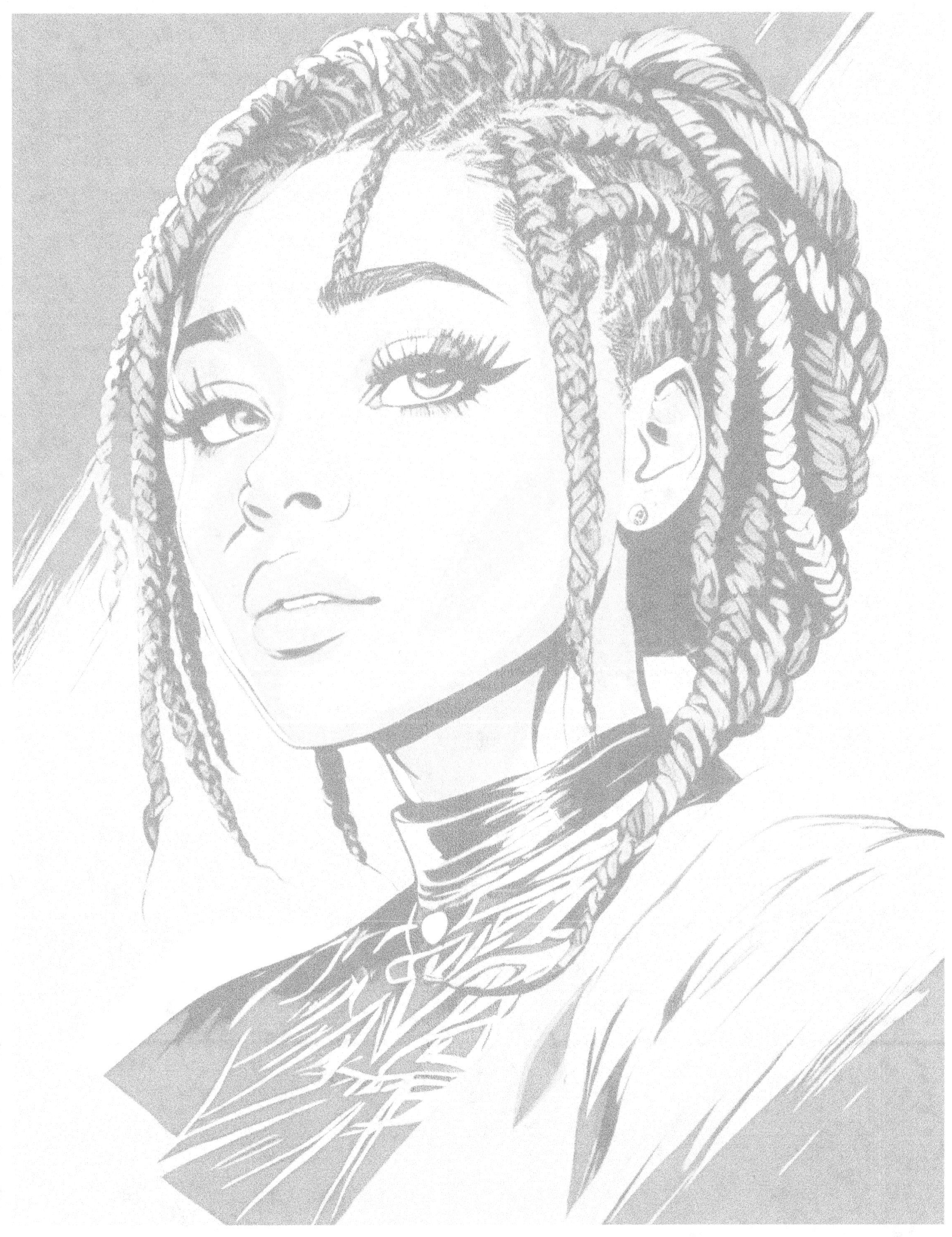

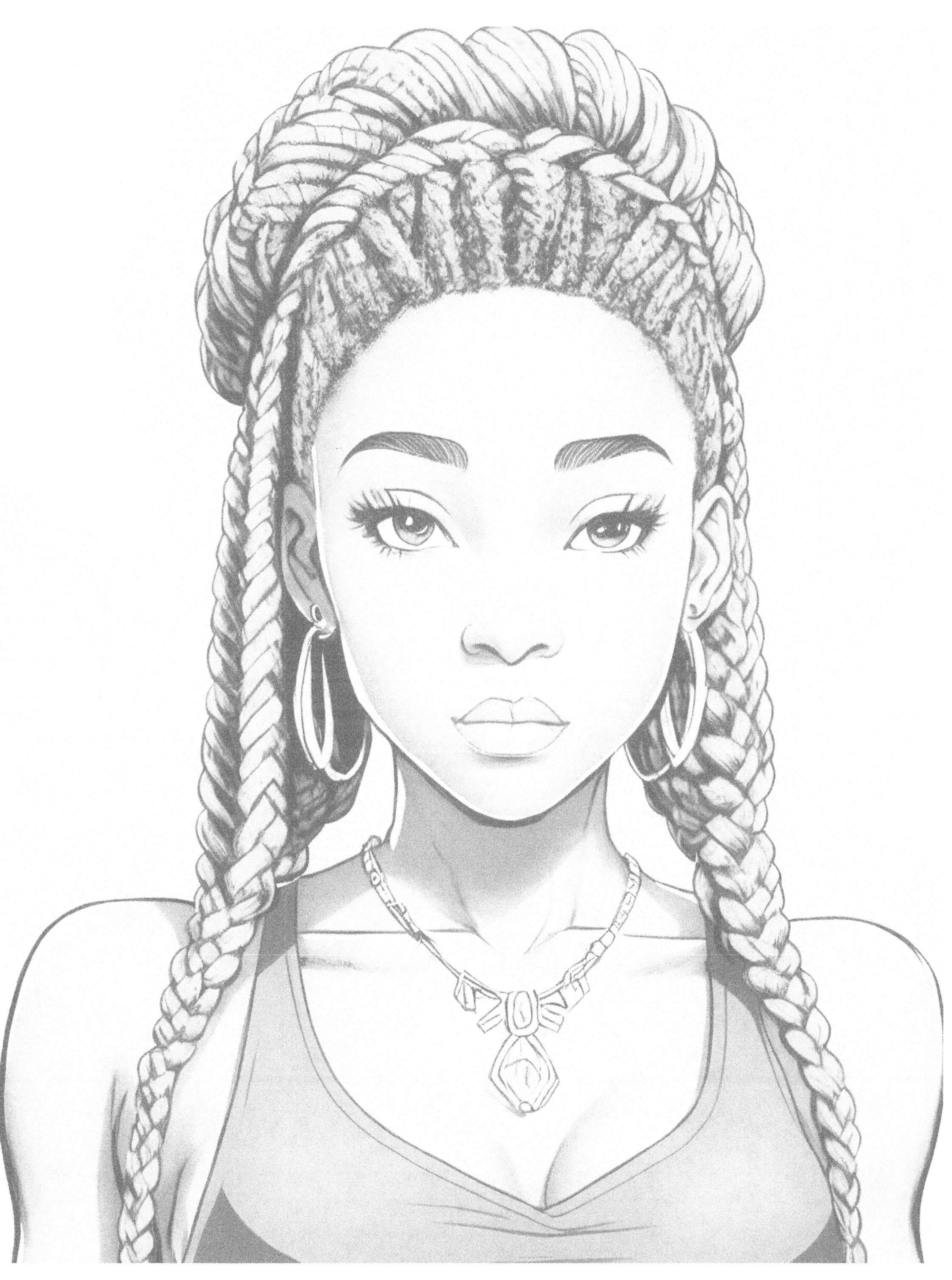

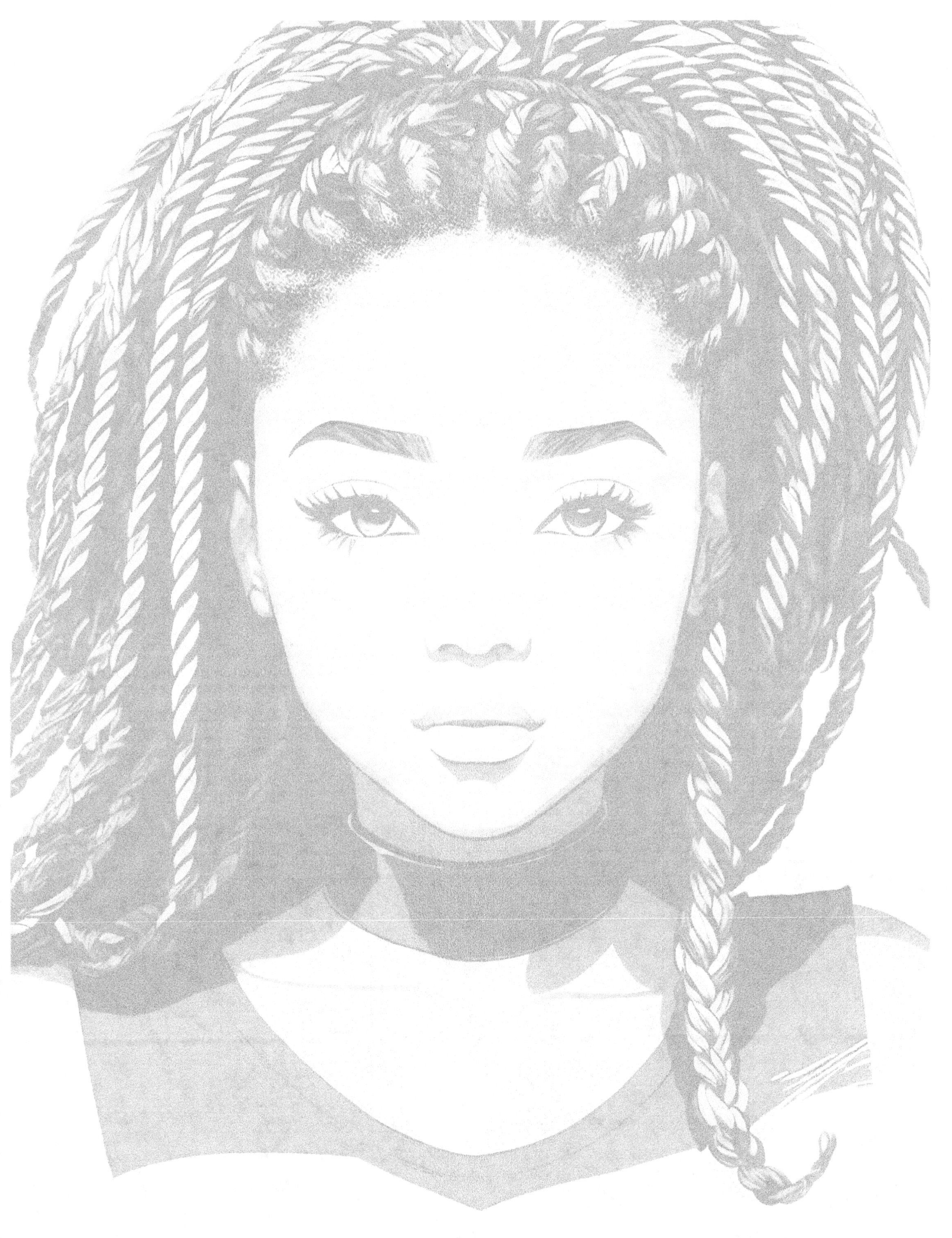

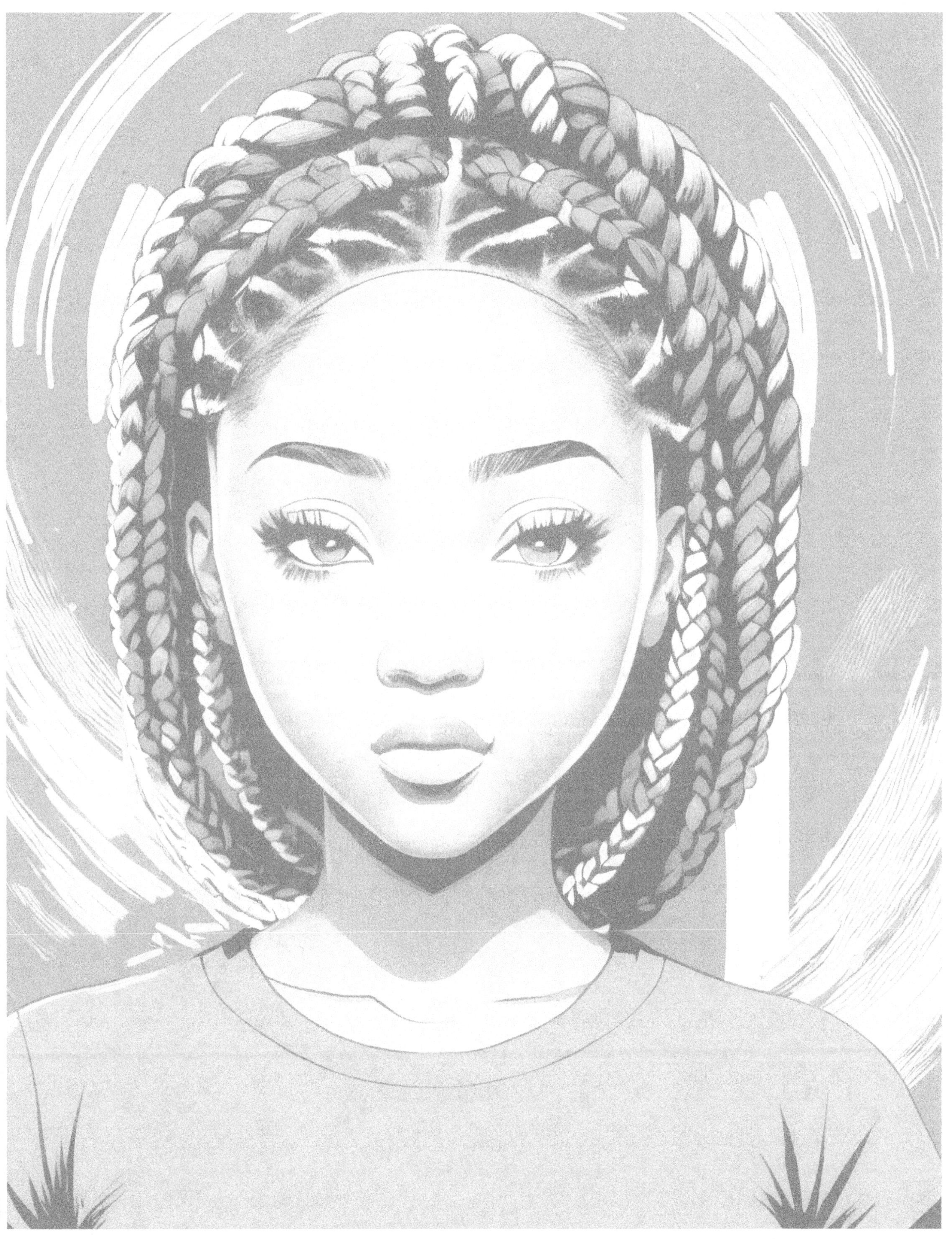

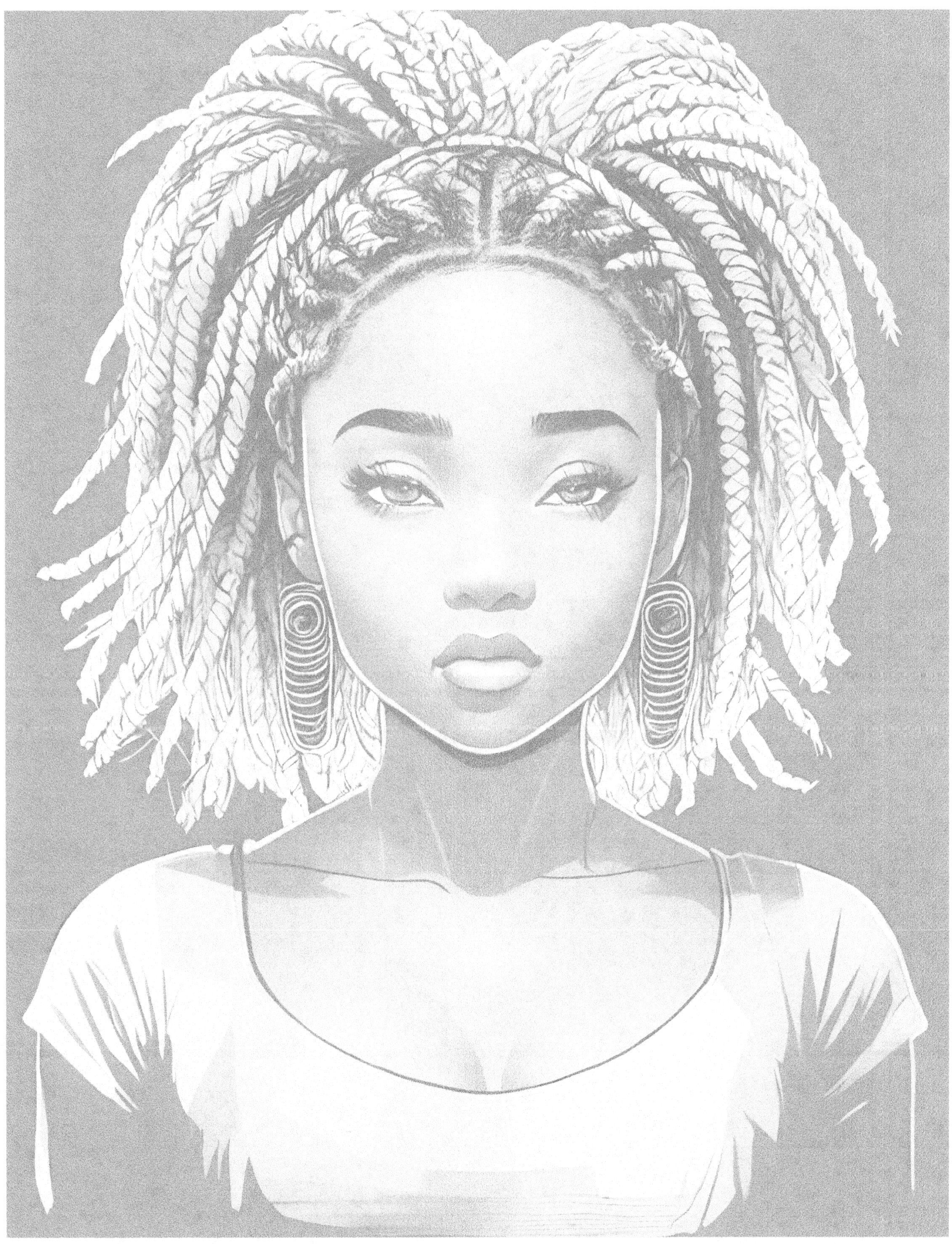

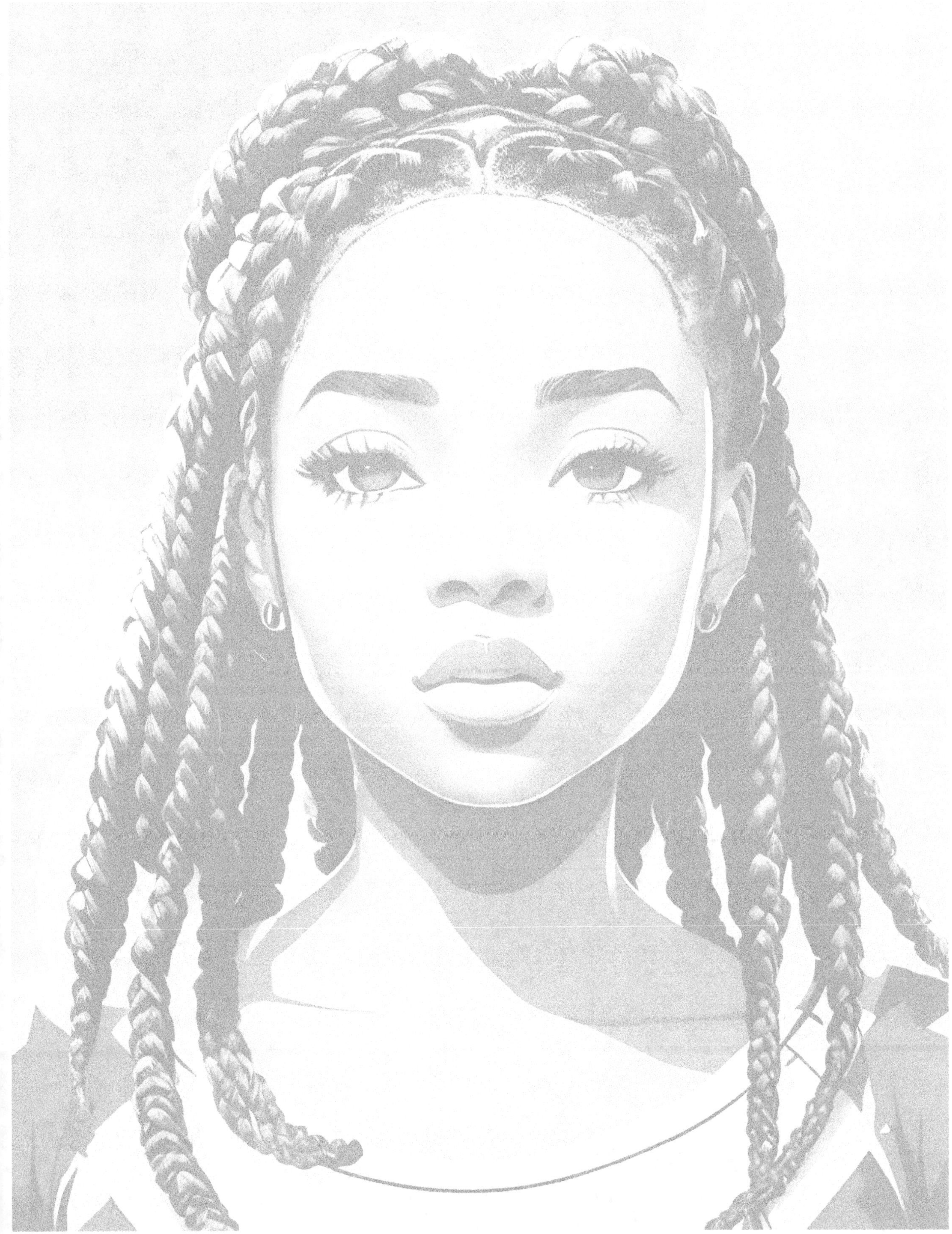

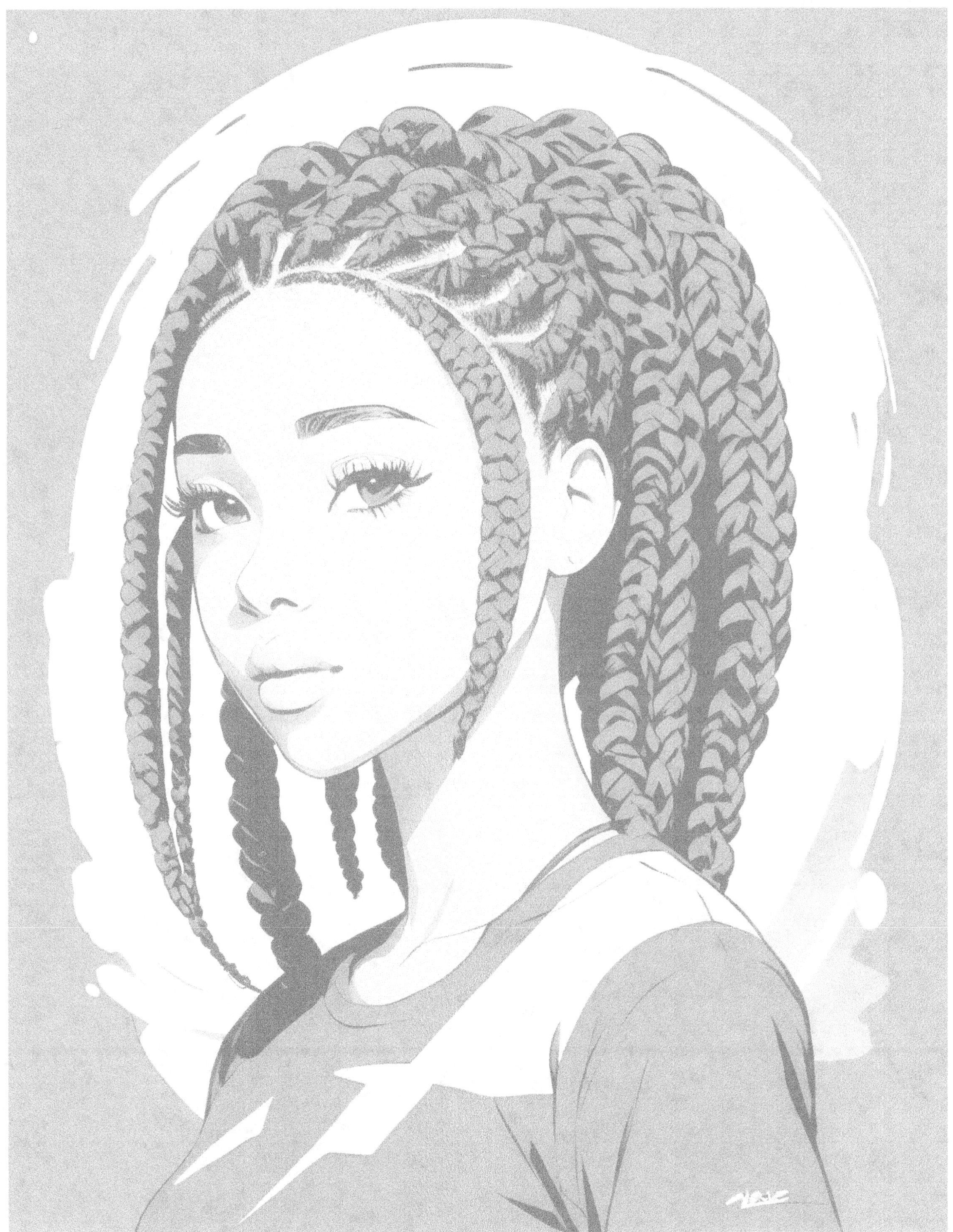

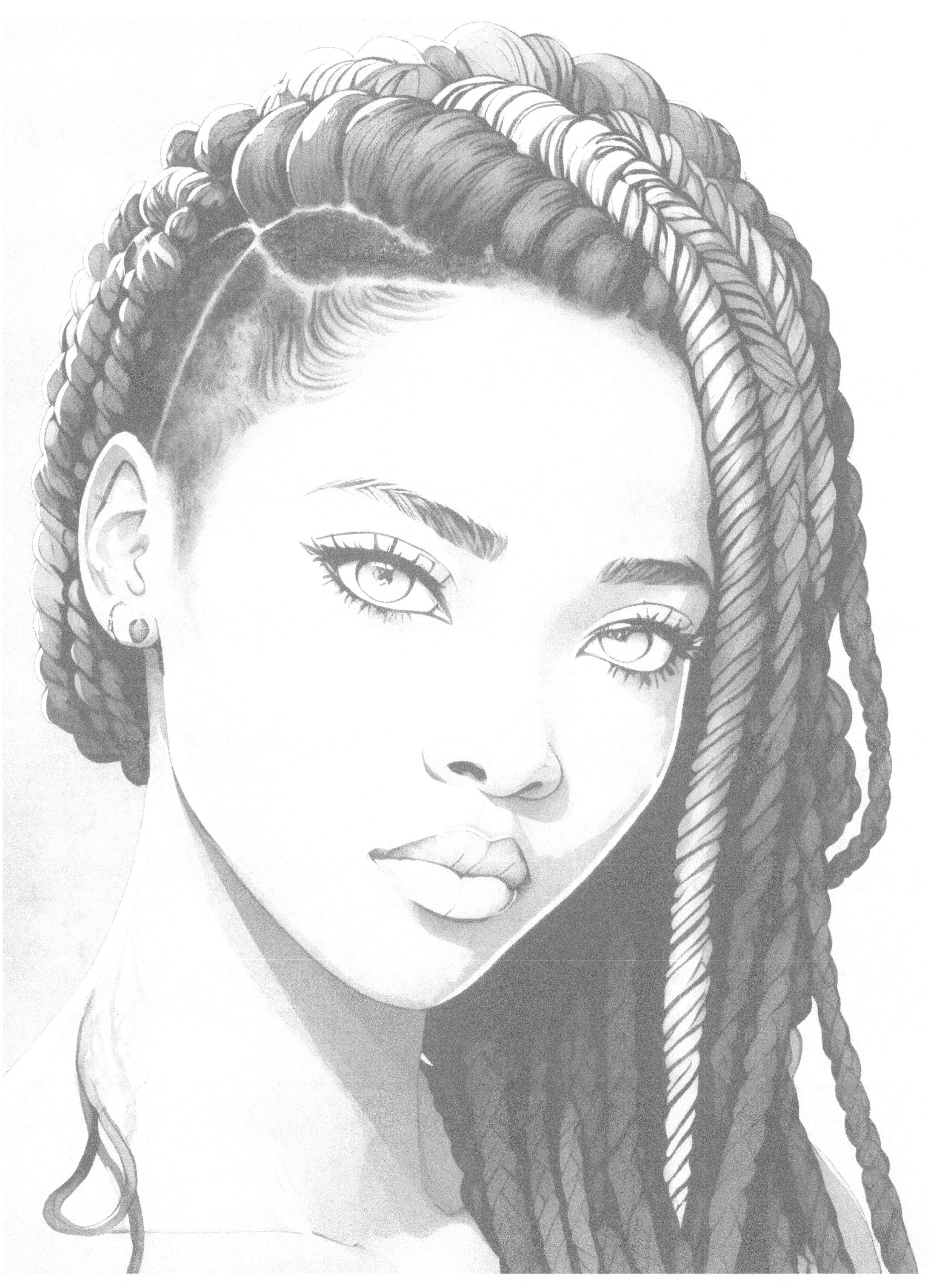

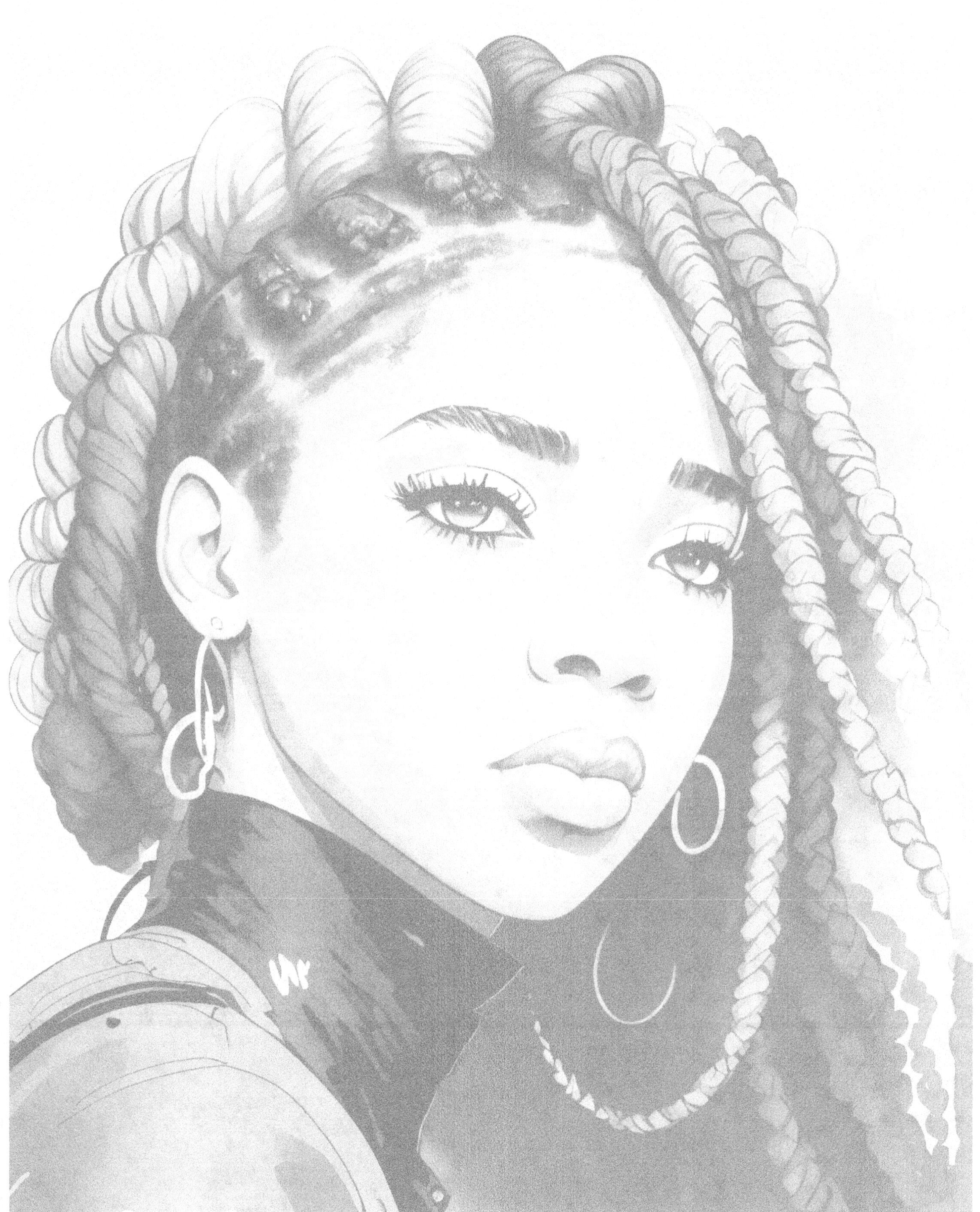

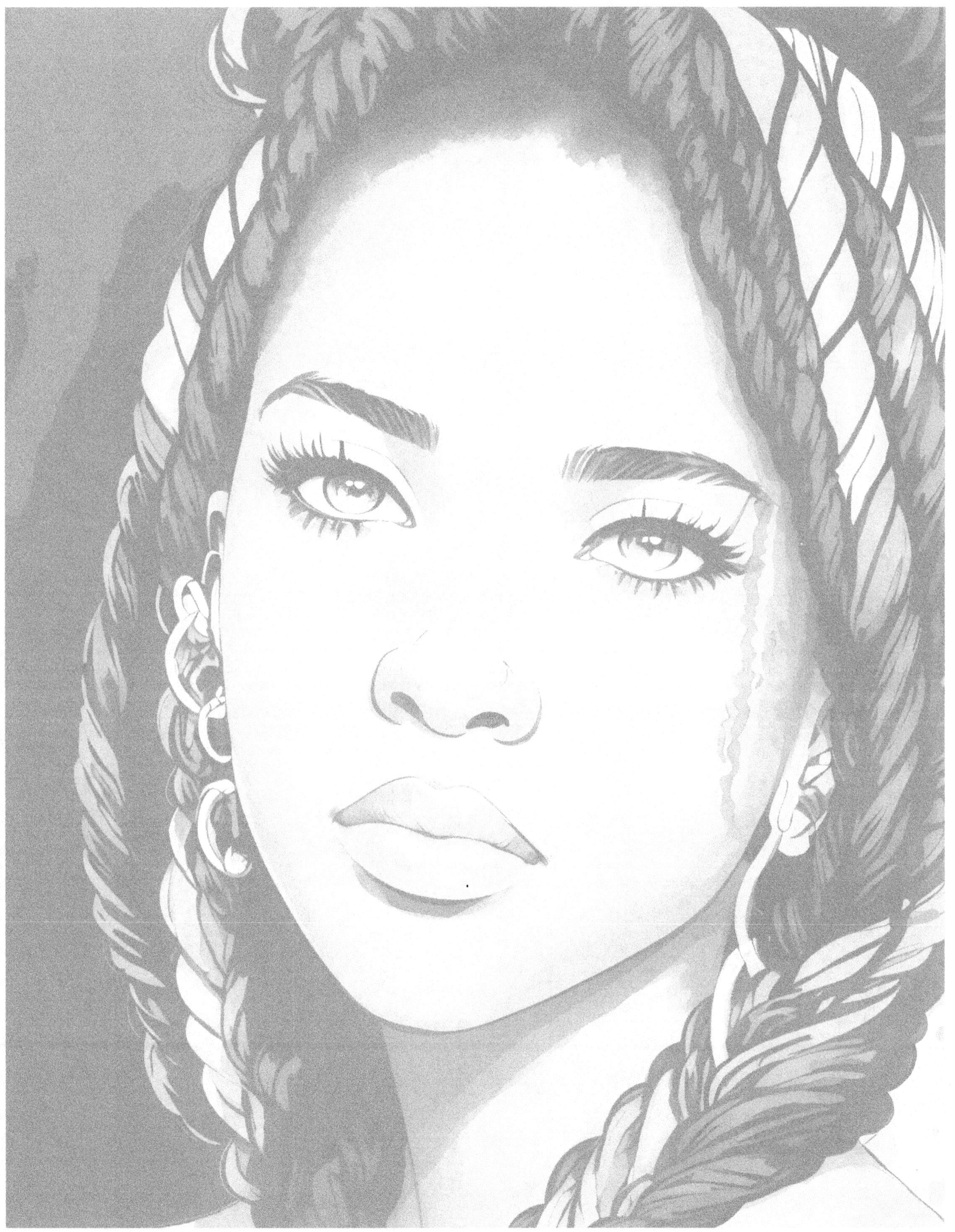

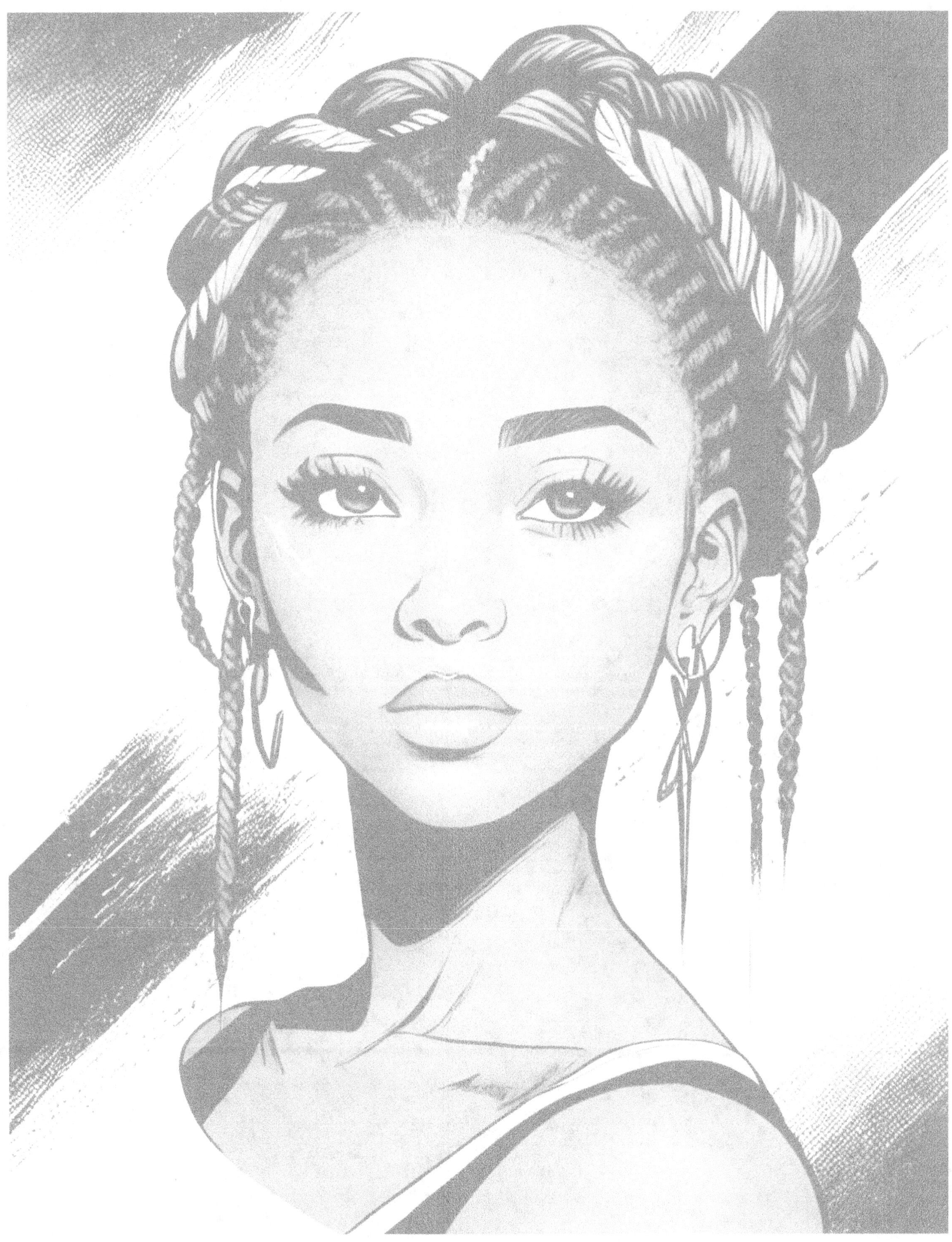

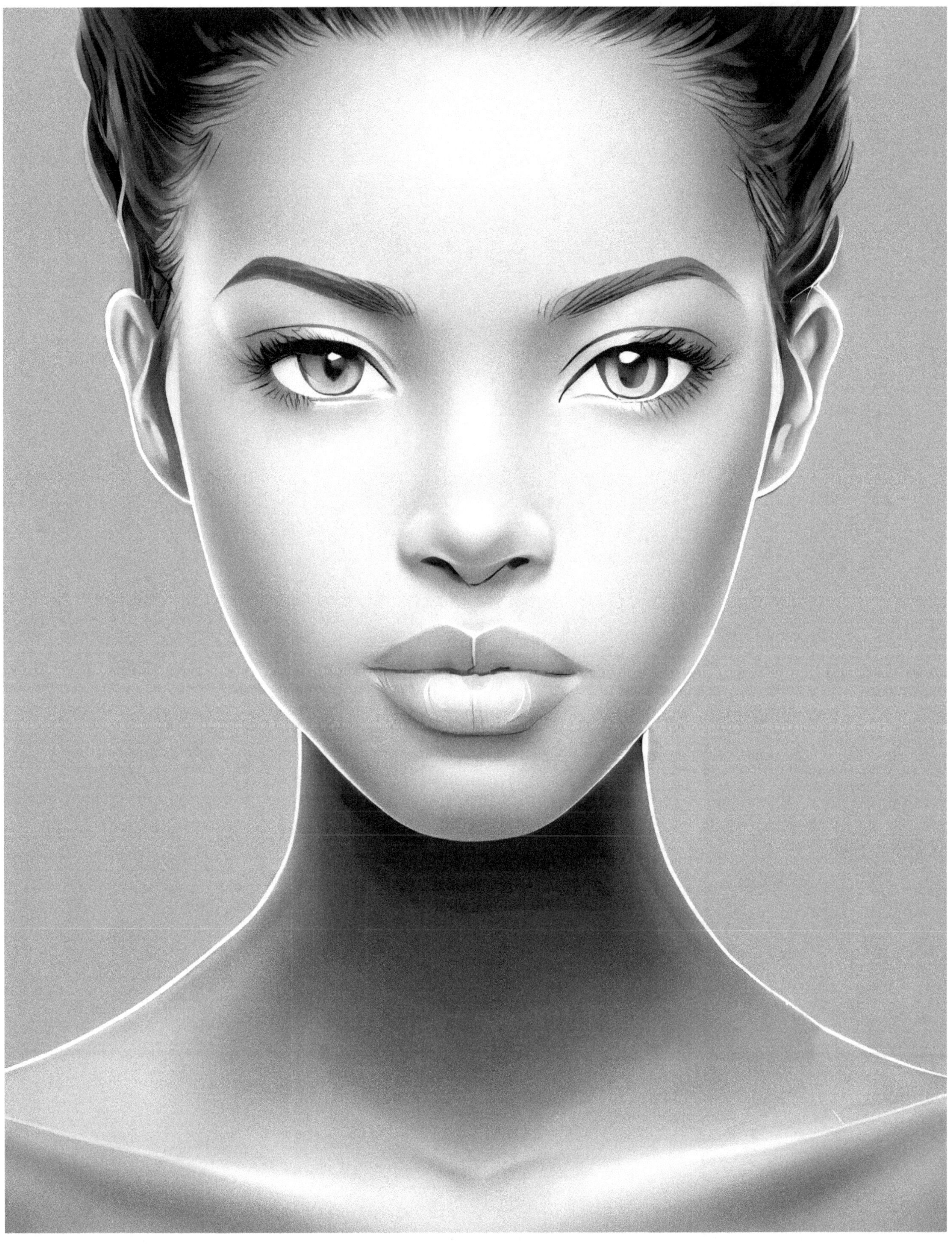

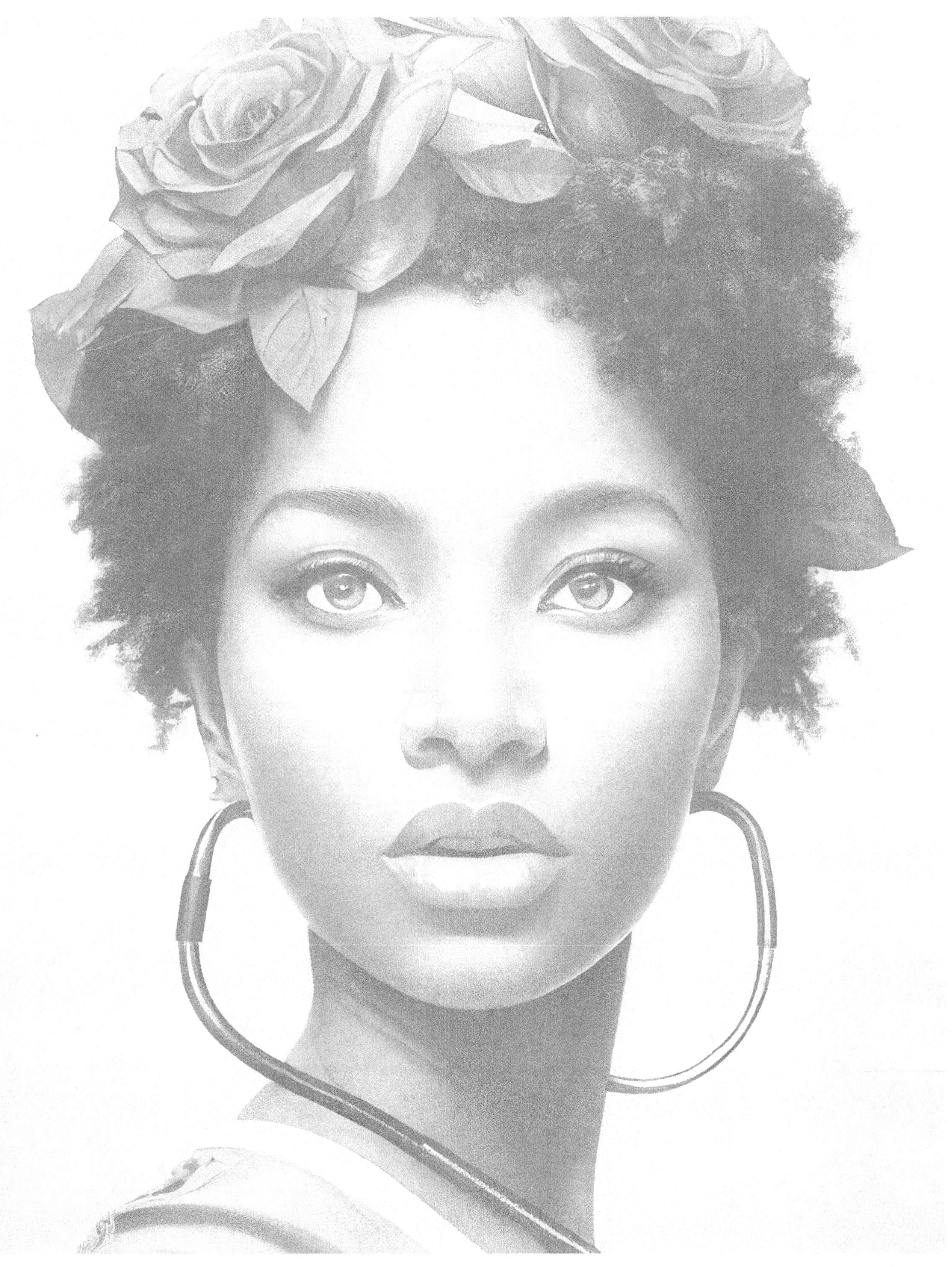

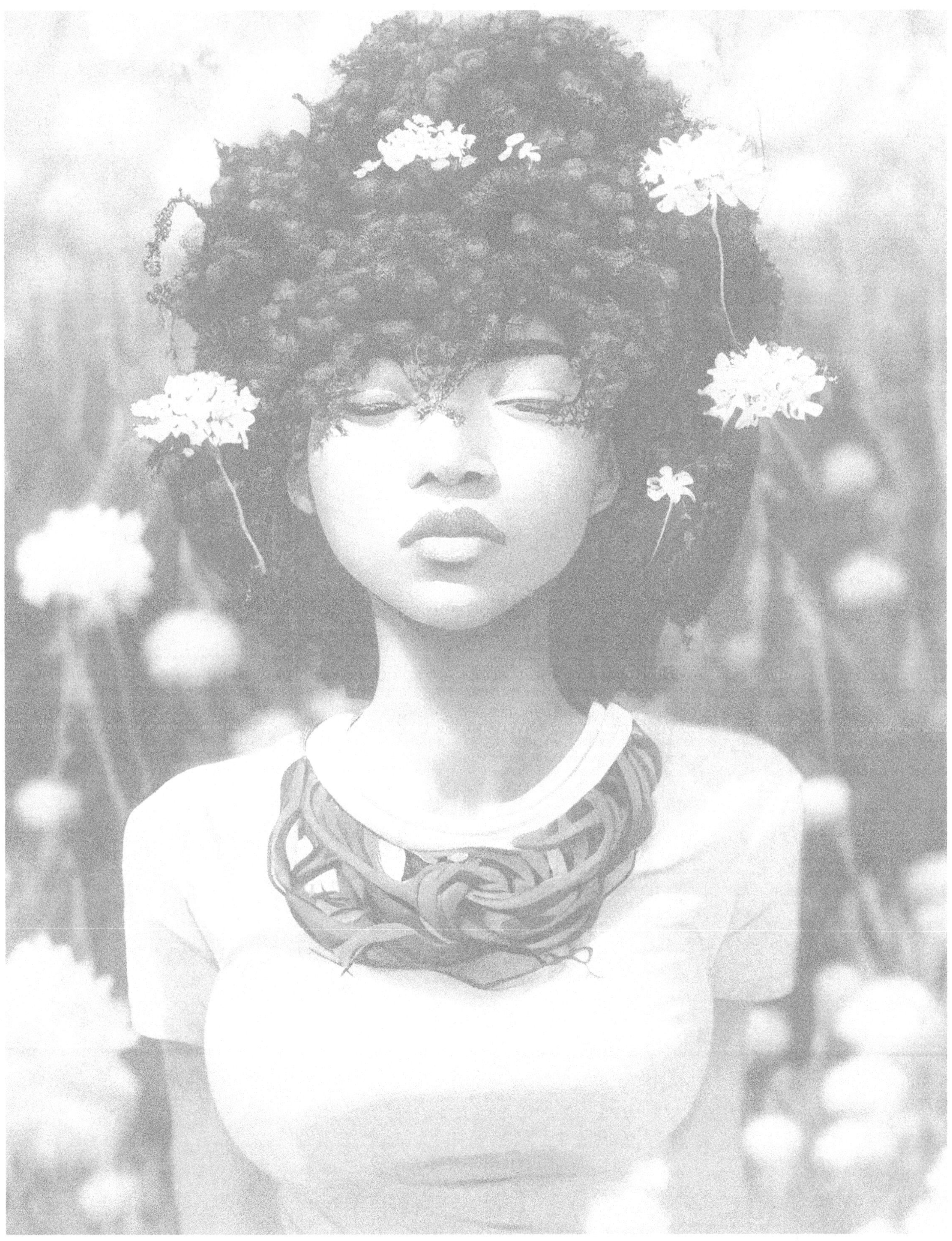

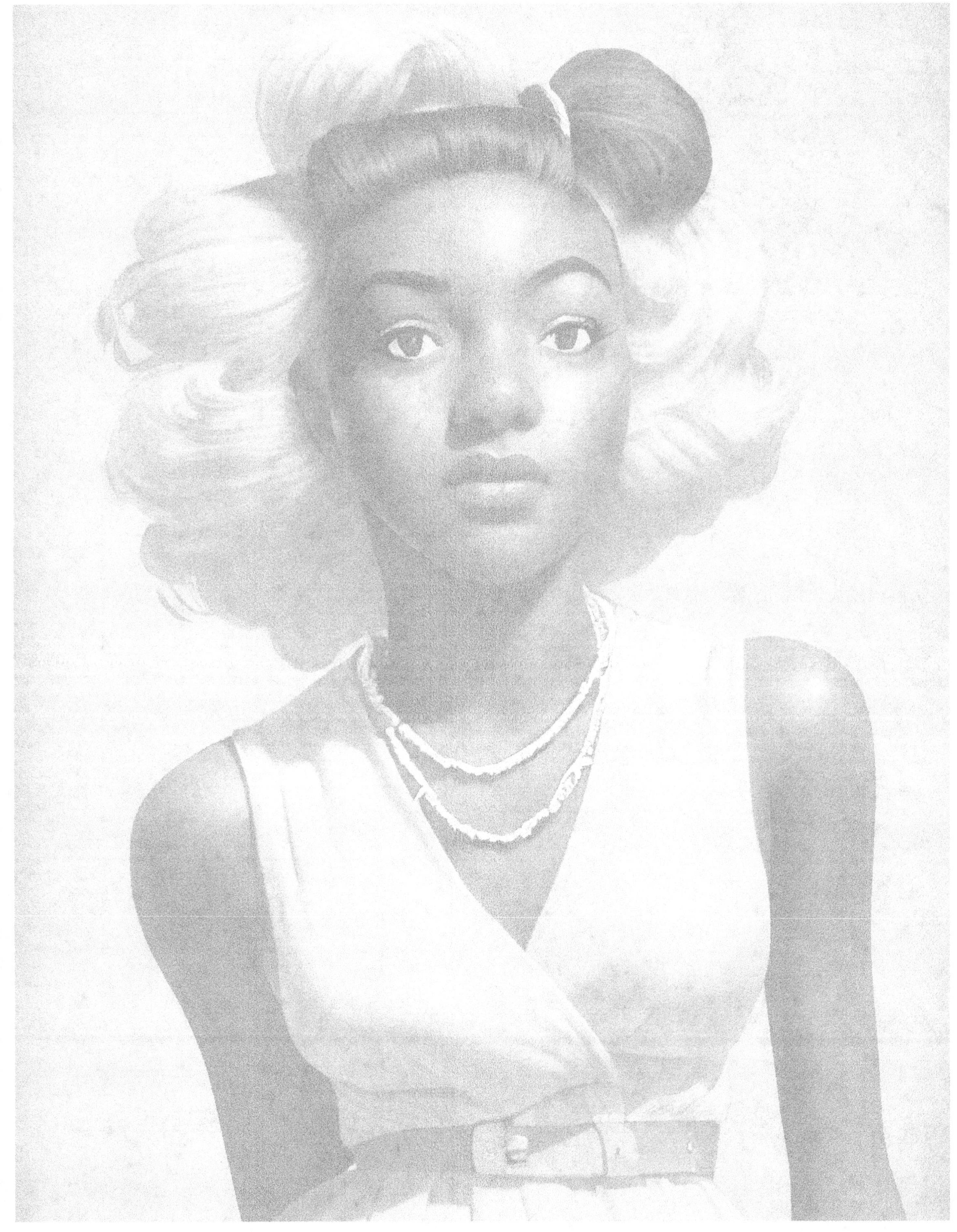

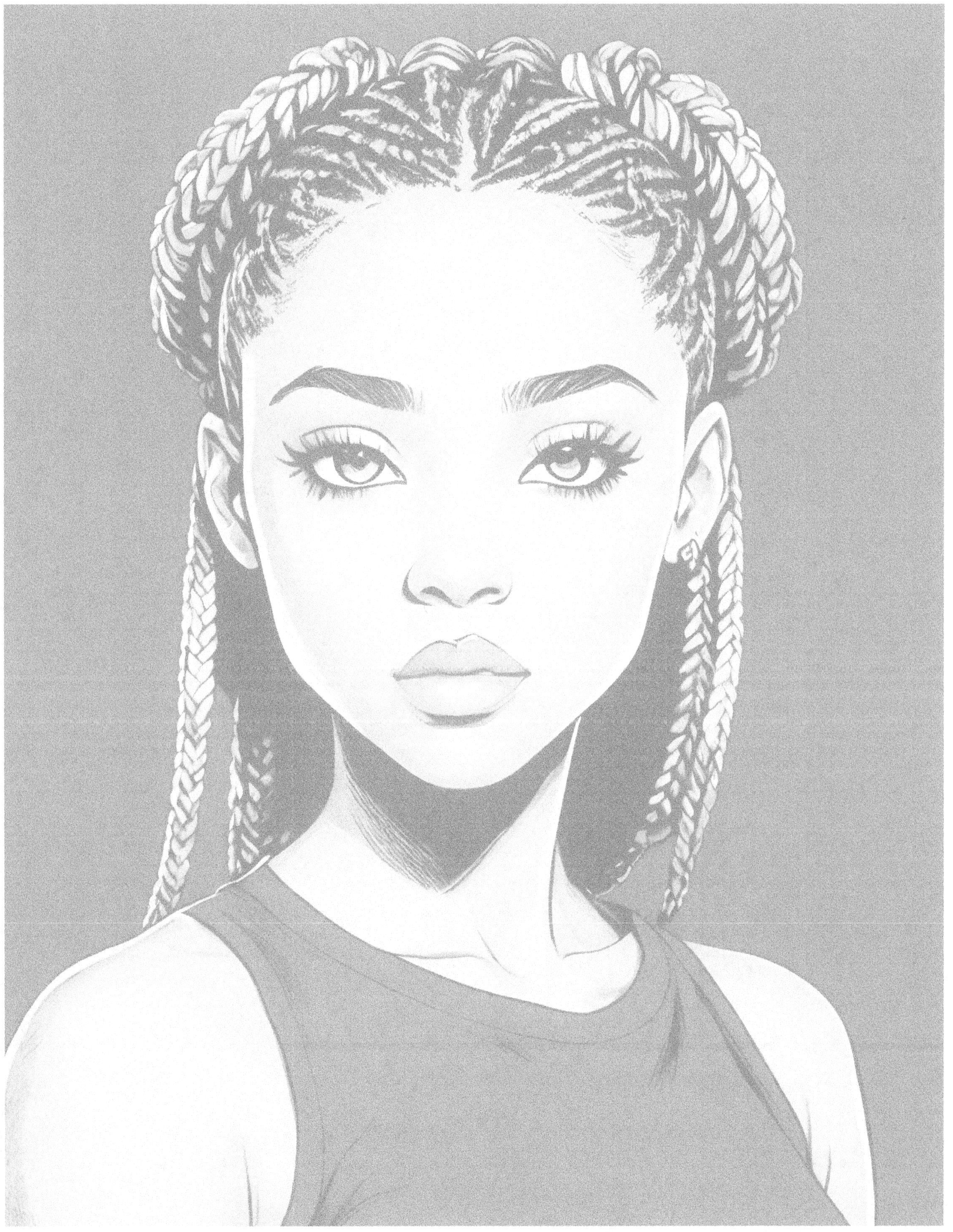

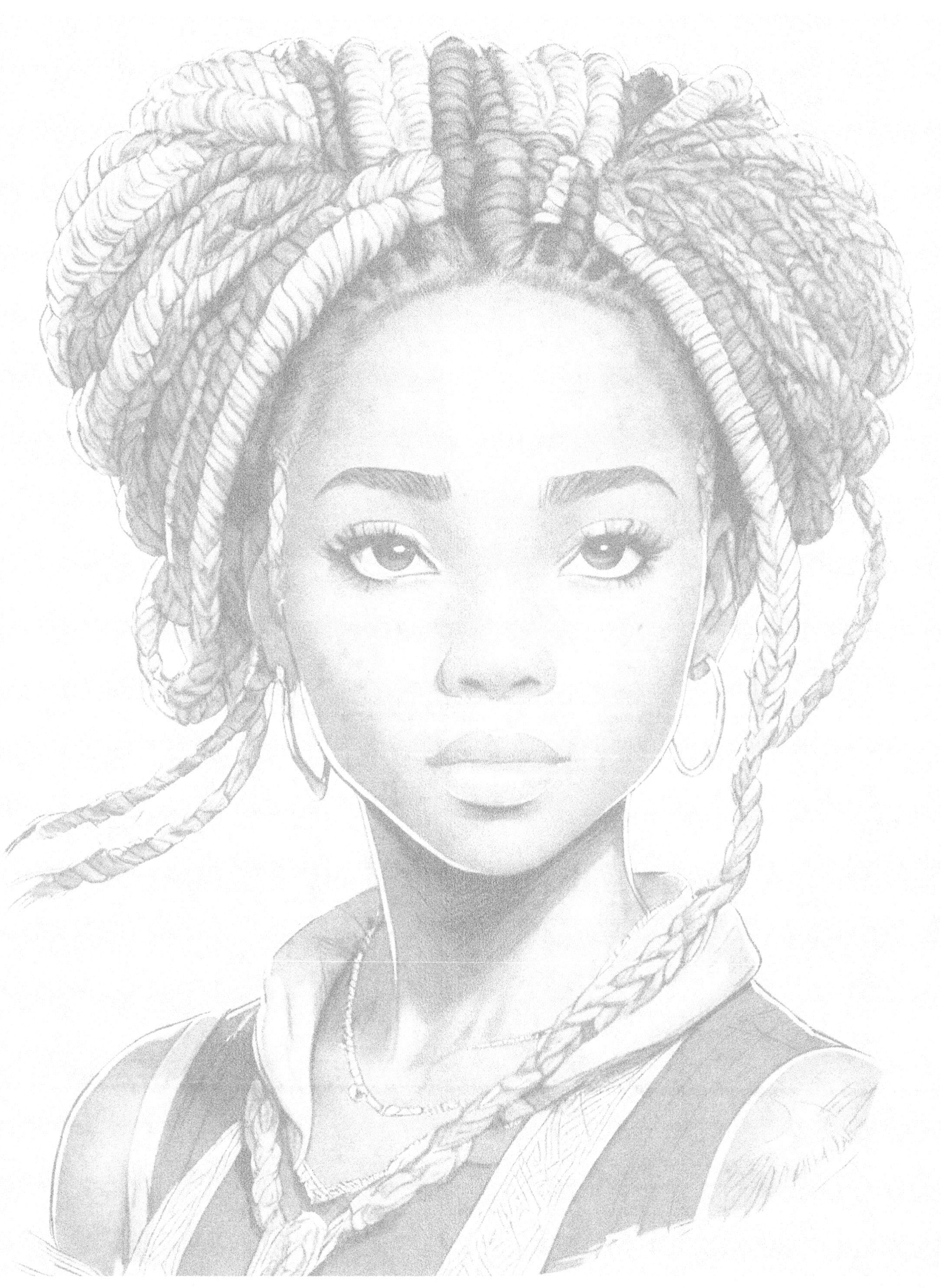

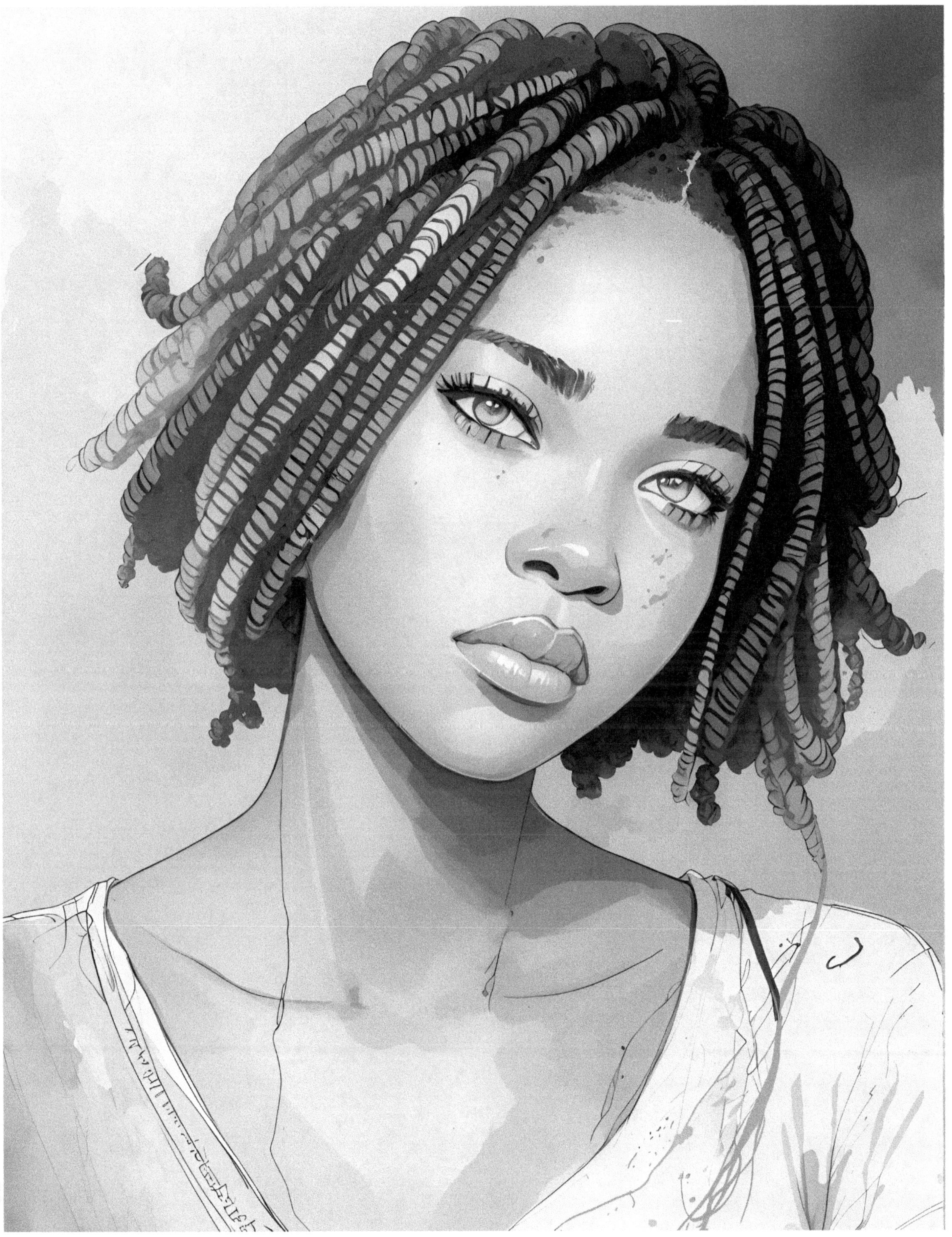

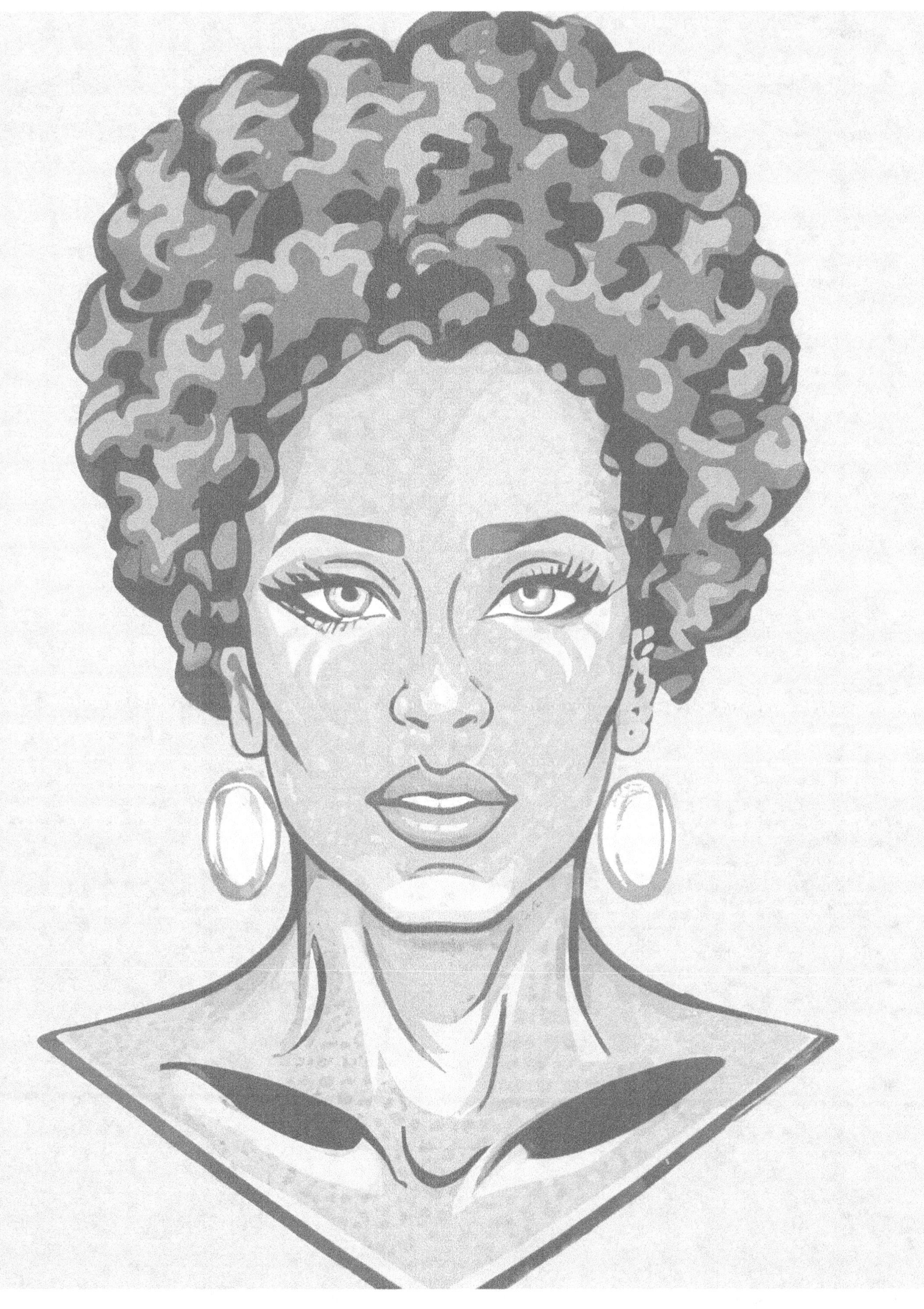

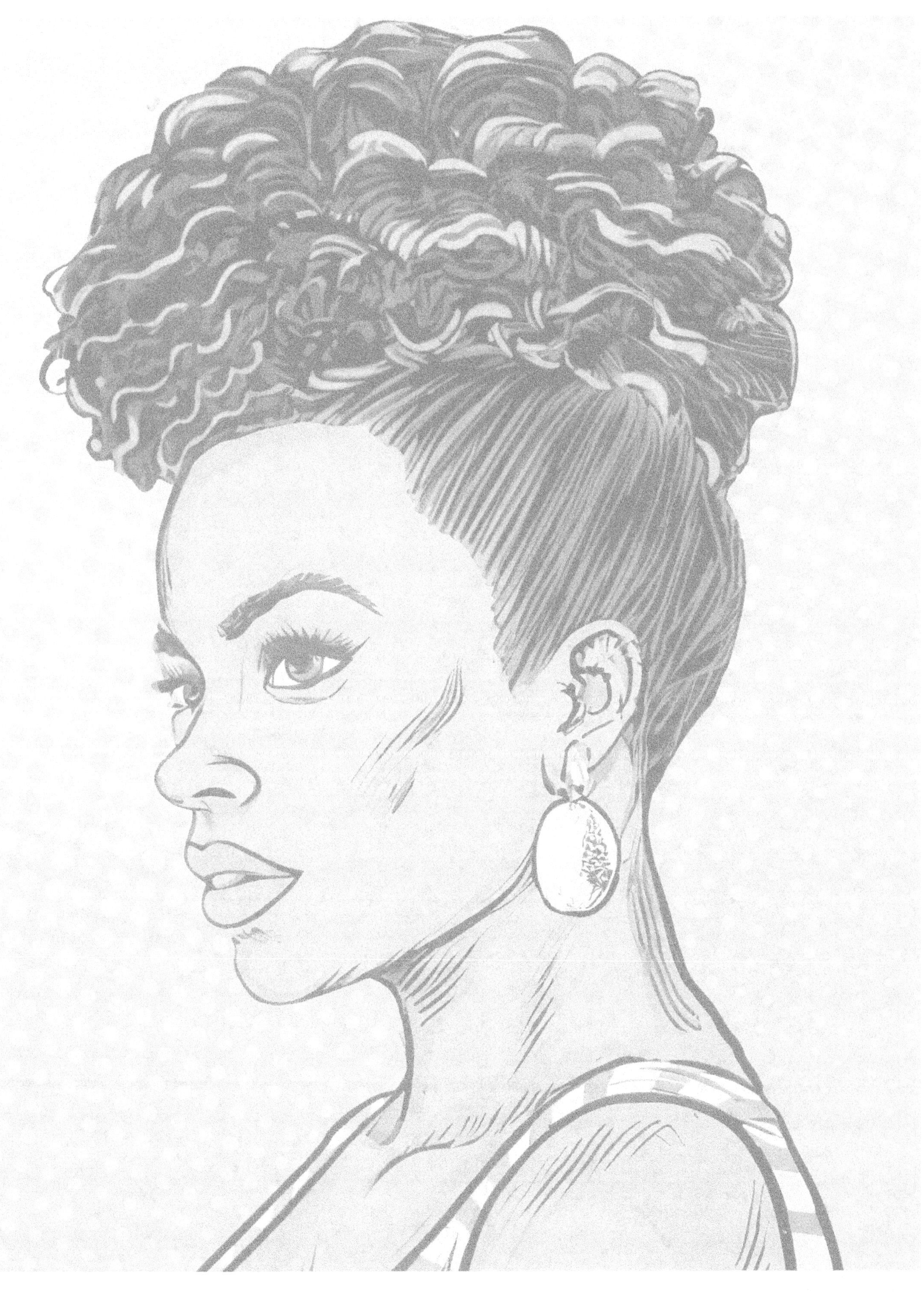

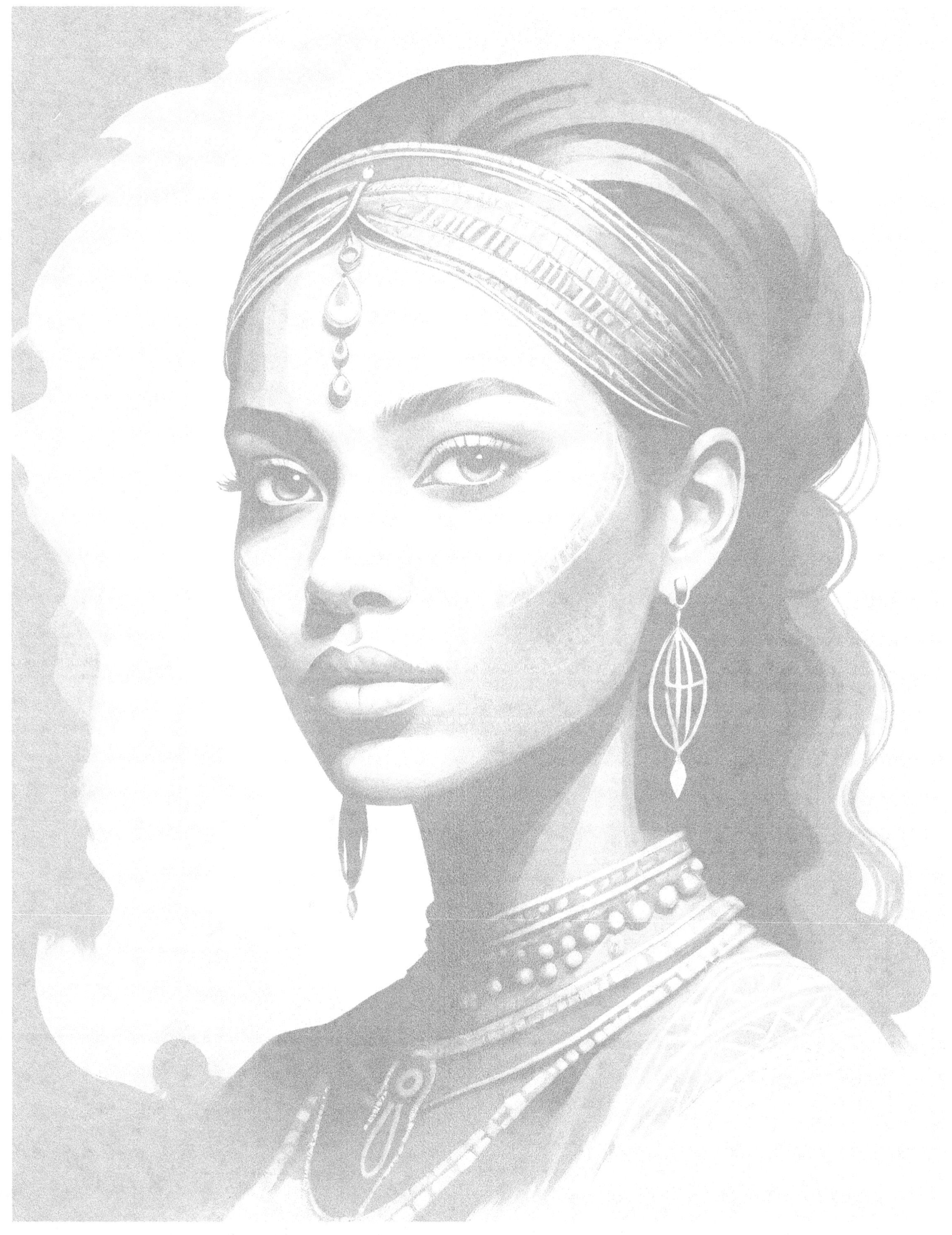

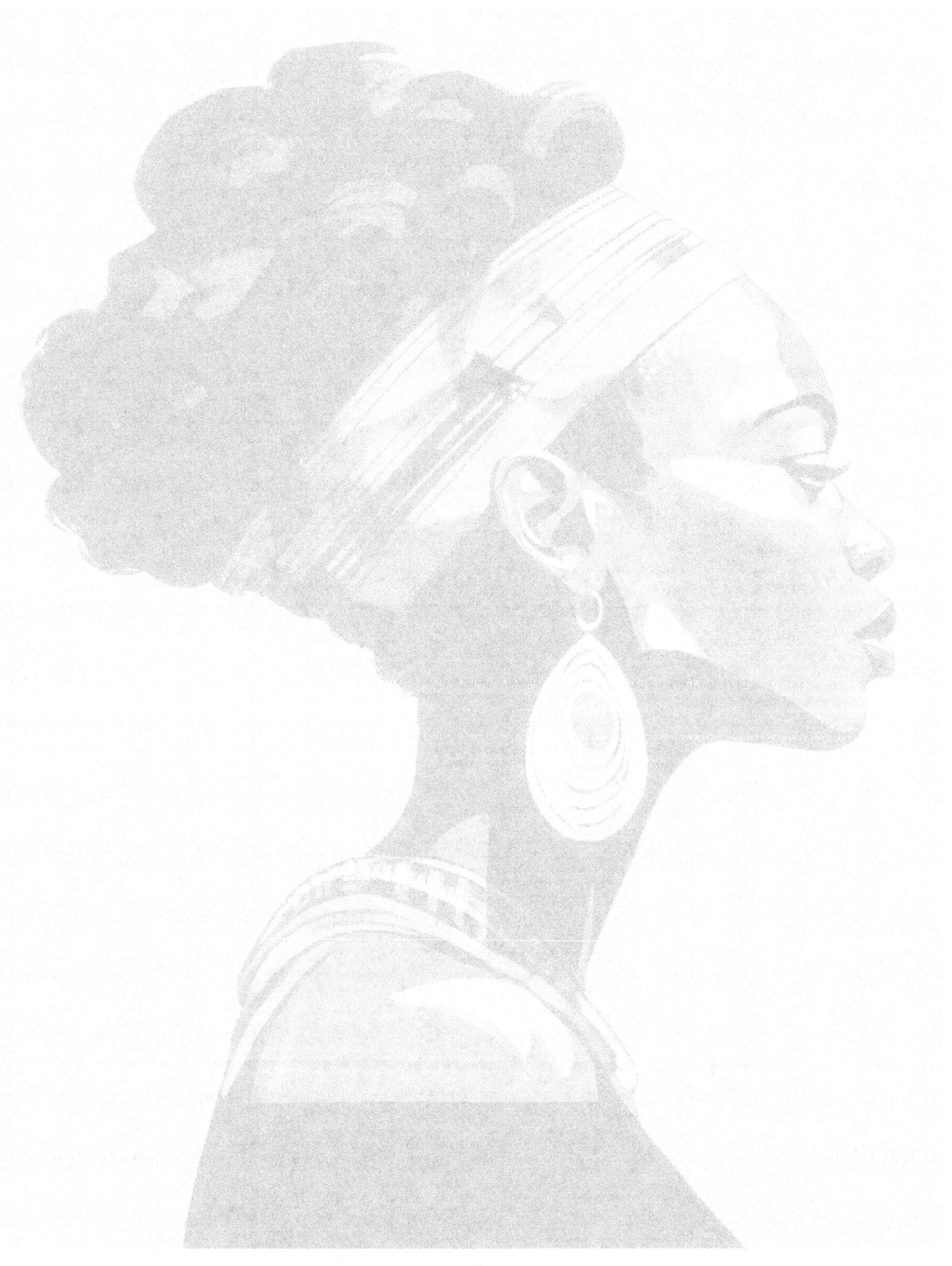

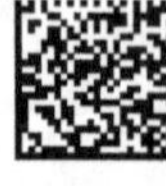